WHERE WOULD I BE WITHOUT ALL OF YOU?

twenty love poems and a song from my bathtub

Lainey Edmunds

BookLeaf Publishing

Presentation by *BookLeaf Publishing*

Web: www.bookleafpub.com

E-mail: info@bookleafpub.com

ISBN: 9789357445504

First edition 2021

come to me

come to me
with all you could possibly bring
come to me
with the scent of past lovers on your skin
with your childhood tragedies at your feet
with a heart so broken
your body can no longer bleed.

come to me

and i will show you no fear. for i too, carry grief
for i too, am broken.

show me your hands and i see no red
show me your heart that can wholly mend
i have been told we are only as brave we believe,
we are only as brave as we believe.

when i look at you, i see intelligence
i see beauty beyond comparison
when i look at you, i see you.

and i may only be a witness to right now

but i can feel you as though you are all i know

and as you come to me
your eyes, brave art
your hand, placed over my heart
you too, can see me
for i will never be too far.

beginning thoughts

my back lies stiff
i hear hummingbirds
buzzing in the tree above me
the blanket i lay upon suffocates me
but only slightly
still, i adore it here
all senses belong to the sun and stillness
the sky is a bright shade of blue today
my arms cross over my sunburnt frame

honestly, i was too high to move
honestly, i was thinking of you

how-
if u were here, i'd let your head rest beneath the warmth of my belly
how –
my fingers would get lost in your long, tangled waves
how-
you watch me and never seem to look away.

you kiss me with sweet intention
always soft, always willing

i have not yet learned what makes you, you
and you do not know me
past late night pleasures
or watching my freckles grow under the sun

but-
i think i want you to.

tangled

my limbs tangle with yours-
tiny, like four buttons i carry in my pocket or the
thin stem of a rose.
you stole my pen to rewrite my next three hours
and i let you.

my breasts against your breasts, my fingers left
wet in your mouth.
far away, the moon convinced you and finally
led your feet to me.

oh, what wonder to know such magnificence.
because of you both, i have become nocturnal.

you have used your limited words to tell me i
can conquer the world
and because of this, i am in love.

breathless

think of the nights that i have left you breathless;
strokes from my fingertips
against your stretched frame,
spelling my favorite words
across your naked rib cage.
i could barely feel you back then.

and now
i have grown to know every inch of you
i own parts of you
as you own the letters that spill from my pen
and the melodic notes that form above my head.

when i hold you, i am holding onto everything.

and i have spent countless days
trying to make sense of what it means to have fallen,
i have spent countless hours
trying to find the courage to tell you

but because of you, i cannot speak
because of you, i have lost parts of me
and i am captivated in this surrendered captivity.

think of the nights that i have left you breathless;
may it be many or several or few
and know-
that everyday, every hour,
every insignificant second
i am not breathing because of you.

bathtub, books & bed

in winter
we run.
a forest, a city, a desert of the whitest day
this tub is a sea
and your knees are the mountains,
i have grown to love you in between my
warmest sheets
after i leave the left corner dripping.

i have grown to love you in winter
as if every season before has only been lust
you must have loved me long ago
or you would be a hundred days behind this one.

my sweet softness, my muse
now,
when i look at you, i see my future.

i thought love could only live between the lost
and unknown
until we found each other
and carefully listened to every word said
just to bend them as beauty.

if one day i shall wake to see you gone
my feet will form weight and i could not run
again.

so, i ask of you
to shelter me in the castles of your arms
let us reach spring, summer, fall,
then winter again
and i will crawl to your mouth each night just to
kiss you,
i will speak words of poetic melody and paint
our future fantasies

spend all your empty seasons with me
and in this tub, in these sheets,
we will run
eternally.

i think of you

when i close my eyes, i think of you.
tonight, yesterday, tomorrow. i think of you.
and the lips that you own,
how they press against mine
and your hands felt wandering up my spine

i do not belong to you- yet.

you see,
i've been scared of you since the day we met
you seem so perfect
and your mind works so different
from mine.

i'm afraid, you're afraid
and you'll regret all the nights you've spent
tracing your fingers
along the soft parts of my neck,
you'll wish away
all the mornings you've woken up in my bed

and i often wonder-
when the heartbreak will begin.

i close my eyes, just to think of you
just to see its truth
just to watch you move

and despite my fears, despite my tears,
i am in constant awe, just thinking of you.

-994 more

she is not the sea or a forest of the finest green. nor a woman so whole she has everyone down on their knees. she is nothing because she is like nothing and when i look at her, i laugh. because i see the eyes of an innocent child or a seasoned academic or someone who just loves every type of ugly art.

you see, there is a folder i keep with every letter of the alphabet and now M can only mean one thousand things;

-expensive electronics
-ratty laced thongs
-leaving a skateboard in my car

-chopsticks flipping chicken at 6pm
-two bodies in the bathtub
-begging beside the word 'beso'
-994 more.

how lucky am i to lie next to another who loves me as though love can only belong to me?

and she would give me everything this world has to offer, except the one thing i want most;

her future.

cause there is a dreamer so big it fills the whole room; city lights mixed with afternoon moons/ bringing to life a forearm tattoo/ a reflection so new that the past and the present splits into two.

i would push aside every element of earth just to stay by her side/ just to watch her blood run quick from obscure topics and altered video clips/ just to look at her lips form the phrase to 'i love you.'

just to gaze at my favorite view.

but no one can break the heavy stream from flowing. no one can hold onto light. no one can stop the ticking hands of time.

and why would they want to?

i have a feeling i will blink and she will be gone and my hands will still reach out because that's what they've done and there will be nothing but emptiness and air where i would reach for her body and play with her hair and i can't do anything but tell myself over and over- this is so fucking unfair.

and everyday something is telling me it has nothing to do with me, yet- i am a small flame when she asked for fire, an unfinished art piece collecting dust in the corner. i am too small too boring too safe to consider and when our final days come to an end i will tell her it was all for nothing and i would take back every moment that ever meant anything and i hate you i hate you- i never loved you.

but she'll know, it's untrue.

cause my eyes will fill with tears reflecting all truth/ between the pain of letting go and the power behind dividing our youth.

and maybe, under all this armor we're just stained in rust.

maybe, we've exhausted all lust.

or maybe, the world isn't ready for something as beautiful as us.

to love you is to lose you

and only as i feel you slip through my fingertips,
i will love you.
as though time is mine and never yours
as though love has never scared me before
and i will act as if i have done no harm
as if your knees have never bled
from begging me to love you.

to love you, my love, is to lose you.

i speak of art beside your name
only ever beside your name
i think, for eternity.
and your body
your body, my love, is leaving me.

i have held your heart for long enough
you will kiss my tear-stained lips until we part
and as my hand leaves your hand
for the very last time
i will look back at you to truly understand

my love, i have loved you all along.

when sea meets mountains

silver foam forms at my ankles. full, stroking.
it makes its bed in contour of the coast.
you have brought me to your home,
haven't you?

tonight, i will watch the stars wrap their arms
around your frame,
the golden sky will take your darkness away.
twilight, your weighted cry.

i have never met a speechless moment until you.

the sea left your clothes to the sand, weak beads
compared to your pale pearls.
i will watch your songlike stir for days
into evening, only writing of your beauty.

you ask me to anchor my words as if you no
longer wish to belong to yourself.
in all my happiness, i will recite my argument
that you hold the universe,
but i could never hope to consume all of you.

you open your basket of fresh fruit, offer me a
peach plucked from your tree
and my lips will stay halfway sweet until you
kiss me.

body of salt, of timeless treasure, of woman. you
are made of the sun and the sea that birthed you
and i am made of the mountains that built me
under the moon.

that is why after summer's last sunrise, i will gift
you my words of our final goodbye.

i long to be near you

my delicate, reckless one.
why do you keep leaving the hands
that beg of you to stay?
you promised me peace and light
of the warmest days, yet-
i am looking at you
and every step closer is darkness.

when i am near you, i long to be near you.
i silently wait for your eternal embrace
and i want you to want it.

do you want it?

i hear your apologies so closely
i could touch them
but i am telling you i will not listen forever
and i will soon love you as light loves darkness,
meeting as shadows at dusk
slowly, fading into nothingness.

thick tree and earth

i watch your tears fall
as a sea within your collarbone
i listen to you paint every word
as if your eyes have never been swollen.
i feel you trace every shadow beside moonshine,
caressing all shades of my copper skin.
i know, you know
that i will never let you in.

your love is the bed i sleep upon each night
and i want to wrap my arms around day
you know i would peacefully leave
if my limbs weren't rooted
in your silent cry to stay.

you're reaching for the soul of a hollow tree,
i am protected by amour, made of my leaves.
and i wish it was different for you, i do.
but there is no amount of moonlight
or whispers in the breeze
that could ever soften me.

we are both too brave
too deep, too dishonest

to face the truth of today.
and through this thirst of thick tree and earth
i love you i love you
that is why
we stay.

listen

the thing is, i do not want you to love me
what i need
is for you to look at me and know
that i am too hard to hold.

you see me as everything i am not
and your language of lust is repeating itself-

listen

i do not want you to love me.

i cannot take care of the limbs that reach for me
or return time after you realize who i truly am.
what i need from you
is to take my sweet kisses as temporary
and i will erase every tangible word
as you say them to me.

i watch as you run to your friends
and melt at their feet to have found
someone like me
while i trip over ex lovers
and barely lit cigarettes.

i am not soft like you, i do not speak like you,
i do not see this world in colored hue.

the thing is, i do not want you to love me.
but my god, i want you to love me.

wedding season

4-

i stand behind the slab of volcanic marble (the
one imported from chile that all the guests ask
about) half listening to someone order a gin and
tonic, half hating you.

you are holding a small fire, moving as an island
with secrets only i know of
and i will follow you for the last time as if you
are captivating. because my god, you are
captivating.

you adjust the microphone three inches too high,
smile in the way that your eyes turn into a half
moon, tell the groom we're ready for speeches
and i hate you even more now.

in every moment that followed june, i wanted to
hurt you.

with your body rooted, palms painted red

with a burning silhouette that led me from
simplicity
i somehow, still
silently beg to feel you beside me.

all night long i am clutching an image.
my teeth slowly
sinking
into the vows of your limited touch.
and i,
the forbidden fantasy,
the one shaped as rejected truth;

i didn't leave because i wanted to,
i left because i had to.

1-

i fix your pale blue bowtie, brush my fingers
along the flat part of your collar.
a sweet feeling of belonging settles into my
belly. sometimes, i think you're the only reason i
like it here.
fair venturer. you are of new, veracious form
i pick you up like a dying rose. vermilion,
crumbling.

crying against clarity. i am sorry.
you watch as your own petals fall to the floor,
just leave them there.
my hand accidentally touches yours; i am twelve again and you are the boy next door.

you worry because this doesn’t seem right.
well, i want to break you.

2-

it’s 2am. the moon is resting above the water.
glistening in a way that’s unforgiving and asking for it, i swear.
it's just us now.

i help with the cash out because despite you being a manager here, you’re not very good at numbers and i’ve finished closing down the bar anyhow.

the door locks behind us.

i look at the sea, swelling in slow interval; i look at you.

'jump in, i dare you.'

my arms clutch the loose fabric of my winter jacket. a dark lead-like sky covers the stars and universe. right now, everything is still against the tide.

your clothes drip off your body one
honeyed
piece
at
a
time
clings to the sand as if they were never meant for you.

tonight, i think i'll kiss you.
3-

a whispered tease turns left at the next light, one hour and there is a sauna in your backyard.a bead of sweat drips down your bare chest. your flesh, golden as a grain of wheat, salty as the sea. nobody is speaking.

i sneak into your bedroom and wonder why a twenty-eight-year-old still lives at their parents.

a crucifix is hung on the wall, a bible sits on
your drawer and honestly, i've never known
someone who loves god before.

the towel you wrapped me in rests below my
collarbone, halfway down my thighs, slowly
unfolding as i climb onto your pillowed bed. you
light a candle.

your lips flicker in my fixed view. ember to
ashes, a formed figure to my emptiness. you
brought me to your beauty and i knew it would
taste like this.

suddenly, we are made of flames and my life
begins to move in retrograde.
my mouth, sewn shut, my hands, tied. and i want
you to use me time after time.

5-

for one hundred and something days, the wind
knew your name next to mine
and i love you god damn it, i fucking love you.

but we are all sorts of wrong, aren't we?
a woman, arm in arm with a woman,
you kissing me all winter
then leaving me for june. well,

you didn't leave because you wanted to.
you left because you had to.

broken girls

and sometimes
on some nights
during certain hours between moonrise and light
i am reminded of the day my island walked
miles to meet yours.

eyes of daunting dusk,
lips made of lies wrapped in trust,
the first time i looked your direction
you told me you thought this was love.

as we laid side by side,
our bodies blindly becoming undivided,
you convinced my darkest thoughts
that i am worth loving.

you confused me with your speech of heat and
hands of haunted rhythm

and what i've learned through divine wander
and streets that lead to destiny,
is that i have never loved you.

you looked into me
and saw everything i've ever been
then, with a deep breath in, you said;

i guess i could love a broken girl.

for years,
you tied my hands behind my back
and only kissed the golden parts
i watched, everyday
as you pointed at the face
of beautiful destruction and art next to art

just to say;

look at me, look at me,

i am love.

and maybe
during certain hours
between moonrise and light
i did love you

and the way you could make me cry
when no one else could
and how when you would scream at me
i would fucking feel something

and your diamonds, your pearls, your unearthed
bones of dust and dirt
i wanted to fall, i wanted to break,
i wanted your hands wrapped around my waist.

day after day we left
and came back to each other.

and maybe,
there is some type of twisted pleasure with
holding on to things we know won't last.
maybe,
i do want to blame everything on my past.

but what i've learned through divine wander
and streets that lead to destiny
is that before you, and after you,
i was never broken.

wouldn't we?

once again, you return and you don’t even ask
as we’re slipping back into the comforts of our
past. slipping back into these heavy hands
heavy heart, heavy weight so heavy i am broken
as it breaks.
well,
we’ll go back to where we were
before the passion died but after the hours of
fear pass by.

and you’ll smoke a pack of cigarettes then sleep
with your friends and i’ll sit silent in the tub and
tell no one it’s over because what if it’s not
over?there are three things i will remember;

- your voice in love
- your touch as my drug
- our final farewellas we finally leave

i mean, we would be fools to stick around,
wouldn’t we?

wouldn't we?

and what is the reality behind comfort anyway?

our love for toxicity? fear of the unknown? the thought of spending every night alone?

i don't know how to love anymore and you love everyone and everything except for me and i am one side of the zipper pulling, ripping, why can't it come up?

come closer, come closer
until we give up.

i have been asked to go

that sun-
that sun is the flame i watched her light at 1am
golden wax,
pooling over my stack of past written poems
sinking as if it's
heavy.
grips to the gravity of burnt chestnut,
i watch
as it glides down the leg of her coffee table
slow, almost
honeyed.

i don't say anything,

i'm supposed to be listening.

-i never listen.

beaming or burning, i don't even know.
but it is still, so beautiful.
quietly letting go of everything it holds,
i can only be bitter in its gentle fall.

my heart doesn’t seem to be beating anymore
and the sky is the same idle blue, yet
messier than the day before.

the street light turns red and
my eyes won’t leave her sight
don’t you see?
i thought i was love until morning.

the cars begin to honk and i am the bluest sky.

i want to be that stack of poetry
i want to feel something pour over me
i want heaviness and heat
i want to call it passion as i bleed.

we are numb next to numb and
someone is yelling at me
but this street is my comfort,
this flame is my home
and if nobody raises their voice at me
it means
i am nothing.

she is looking at me, saying something
the wax has touched the floor
and i have a feeling i won’t be here tomorrow.

i walk
as if i don't know who i am
or where i am going
i leave
as if i have been asked to go.

-i have been asked to go.

and i do not know how to be alone
or cry next to nobody
or lay next to nobody

i am nobody

but a girl, silent on the sidewalk
looking at everything she used to be
the sun, the flame,
every poem that came from my name

i was love until now
i was numb until now
i was her everything until
i was not allowed.

the day is now dark and i am lonely.
dreaming of every street our feet has touched,
counting every sun fall we have ever watched

wondering how many words i have missed
through it all.

i light a flame at 1am
tonight,
i know heat of hottest
i am listening to nothing,
to nobody.
i am so lonely
but i
can finally feel something.

reaching

i see you. a million different moons,
all reaching for day.
you say i couldn't possibly know
what it is to be lost
the way a seed seeks its soil in winter,
the way fruit longs for sugar in unfinished wine.

my love, i know what it is to be lost;
i have been following you for some time now.

and i have stripped myself of everything that
makes me whole
my body is your body, my mind not my own.
and when all gravity shakes from each step that
you take, i convince myself it could never be the
fault of a wounded soul.

in me, i hold a yellow sun, growing with its light
the way an unfinished book can soon call itself
an odyssey, the way an apple forms from a tree.

you tell me i must reach
or i will never find my way.

my love, you should know by now,
the moon never meets day.

i hate you

candles flicker in flow of club lights
almost obsolete, almost
like me
and you look too beautiful
to look away this time.
i watch as if minutes are days,
your lips don't belong to his
i thought, like before, you are mine.

i'm angry and you just don't get it,
i'm screaming and you are my greatest storm.
concrete, ivy, ten shades of red
anything but my body belongs to this brick
you paint me with bruises of three dots in a row
and i am already trembling in memory of this
moment.

it's 3am, let's go home.

i am looking down over you,
black eyes of light blue
my hand fastened between your thighs
i only kiss you because i want it to be
our last time.

and by morning, you won't remember
and it's my fault you did this, i know.
if i was less jealous or less insecure
maybe i'd laugh the way you have
but when i tell you i love you
what i mean is i hate you
and if i'm being honest with myself,
i hardly know who you are.

it's been a year of you copying my every move
you now speak the way i do,
dress in my clothes
you live down the street from me
and i want to let go
but you need me, don't you?

in a world full of lies,
at least my last words should be truth;

i hate this, i hate us, and i hate you.

please let me go

flushed and florid
a rouge of the sweetest wine
you've brushed your hair today,
pinned it back how i like.

your tears have cut your cheeks into halves
again. i know you too well to not know where
you've been.

everything rests between your fingertips and
thumb, i have been writing circles all morning.
the space which lets me
be me
left a long time ago

i love you – please let me go.

my back molds to your mattress one last time
i want you to kiss me, even with tears in our
eyes
i want to relive six hundred and something days
all at once

i want to feel your skin as if it has not been
touched.

you lay me down and suddenly
you are nothing.

silk silhouettes, skin of the finest, twisted in a
dark broken breeze.
stillness, two hours away from me and i stare at
the ceiling like i am finally bored.

how is it that you are the only one who can set
me free?
you have seen every part of me and know every
trivial need.

you've been promising too much while taking
another's secret touch
and i'm so tired of ignoring the truth that
belongs to us.

i should have left long ago

i love you – now please let me go.

i, am love

i have spent most of my life living as though i
am lost.
i just like it there.
tiny hands, drawing pictures out of steam in the
back seat
red lights, rainy nights and my mother is yelling
about something.
i am asleep.

i was seven when i first believed that love does
not exist.
ten years of 'we're leaving each other,' well just
fucking do it.
i'm eight and it will always be my fault.
the police are at my house again.
i'm trying to sleep.

concrete pebbles pierce the heels of my feet, i
am running fast this time.
i know i will be back after the street lights turn
bright
after the screaming has stopped, after my
swollen eyes run dry.
i have nowhere else to go

i just want to sleep.

sixteen and a handful of pills finally make it
down my throat.
i want to give up on account of escaping myself
of hating this town, of living a life knowing
there's no such thing as love.
i close my eyes knowing i might not wake up.
please god, i want to wake up.

twenty-two and i write lengths of the lost
i am trying, but not hard enough.
i am looking at a woman, eyes of gemstones,
skin of clouds
and she could be love, but for someone else.
why am i so tired?

my palms are resting down beside my thighs
my heart is constantly racing, my mind a mess,
the world can know my secrets up to twenty-six
but damn it
these walls are love, this pen is love, every letter
tattooed on my arm is love.
i, am love.

a song from my bathtub

she climbs into my body. bare,
a stripped branch shivering.
her words leave, left. a simple touch stretching.
i beg her
time after endless time
for her skin of snow, cheeks of blushing rose
to lie here. to breathe, with me
as a moonless tide, as a flame in subtle breeze
because with her, and only with her

i am beauty.

her knees lean limber
breasts wet, weightless.
she sips my repeating warmth, spits it out,
cries over a sunset she watched three years ago,
sits in silence over an artist who touched her
after she said no.

for hours
i have allowed her hands to fall heavy in my
hands
for years

i have watched every thought brand her skin
from innocence
and to unearth the ability for one to see her as
weak-
it's the closest thing to death there could be
and yet-

i love her and i think she loves me.

here, she brings me things
at morning, at midnight
violin strokes, candlelight.
the slight rouge of rossese,
a spilt cloud at the surface-

the girl who sometimes speaks spanish.

and with her eyes closed,
she holds onto moments of day
and with her eyes open,
all focus drifts away. you see-
i could go so far to say i know her
more than she knows herself.

and while i am only a bathtub
i think *-no-* i know
i am the only thing in her life
that does not resemble danger.

www.ingramcontent.com/pod-product-compliance
Lightning Source LLC
Chambersburg PA
CBHW051741130826
49812CB00033B/955
* 9 7 8 9 3 5 7 4 4 5 5 0 4 *